ULTIMATE SPORTS

DIG DEEP!

EXTREME LAND SPORTS

CHERITON
CHILDREN'S BOOKS

Published in 2024 by **Cheriton Children's Books**
1 Bank Drive West, Shrewsbury, Shropshire, SY3 9DJ, UK

© 2024 Cheriton Children's Books

First Edition

Author: Sarah Eason
Designer: Paul Myerscough
Editor: Jennifer Sanderson
Proofreader: Katie Dicker

Printed in China

Please visit our website,
www.cheritonchildrensbooks.com
to see more of our high-quality books.

CONTENTS

DIG DEEP!

Our planet is amazing. It has mountains, **deserts**, and more, and all of these incredible land features are a paradise for people who love **extreme sports**. These adventure seekers climb Earth's majestic mountains, then **abseil** off them. They find the world's steepest cliff faces and put their bodies to the test as they **scale** them. And they run, bike, skateboard, and more across our world's lush landscapes—the ultimate training zone for Earth's **elite athletes**.

READY TO EXPLORE THE EXTREME? THEN, DIG DEEP AND HIT THE GROUND!

THE EXTREME DREAM

For centuries, people have loved land sports—from climbing and running to cycling. But today, technology has taken our love of land sports to a whole new level. People have invented bikes and boards to use when racing across Earth's surface. We have equipment that helps us scale our planet's incredible heights. And sport science has helped us hone our bodies to endure some of the most **grueling** activities on land. We are climbing, running, biking, and doing more than was once dreamed possible. We are taking land sports to the extreme.

CHAPTER 1

HIT THE GROUND RUNNING

Running is one of the most natural physical sports of all, and around the world, thousands of people do it —for fitness and for fun. But some runners take the sport to a whole new level. They run incredible distances and sometimes, across really challenging **terrain.**

Marathons can be run on roads or off-road, on **trails**.

TO THE LIMITS

For most athletes, running a marathon is the ultimate challenge. The marathon is a long-distance race, covering just over 26 miles (42 km). It is a race of **endurance**, both physically and mentally. It takes the average marathon runner around 4 hours to complete a race. However, the world's elite marathon runners finish them amazingly quickly, often in less than 2 hours!

FIT FOR THE RACE

Marathon runners put in hours of training to get their bodies fit for the grueling race. They gradually increase the length and speeds of their runs, until they are marathon fit. Training for a marathon is a real commitment—it involves hours of running every week for many months before a race.

"RUN, WALK RUN—JUST DON'T GIVE UP."

ULTRA TOUGH

If marathon running is tough, then ultramarathon running is in another league. For some extreme runners, a marathon is just not far enough, and they run distances that vary in length from 31 miles (50 km) to more than an incredible 200 miles (322 km). These superlong-distance runs are known as ultramarathons.

RUN, STOP, SLEEP, REPEAT

Ultramarathons that cover really long distances are often broken up into sections, called stages, so runners can stop and sleep during the race. Most of these endurance races take place on mixed terrain, including roads and trails.

EXTREME HISTORY

Marathon running dates back to the time of the ancient Greeks, more than 2,000 years ago. The race came about after a Greek soldier named Pheidippides ran from the Battle of Marathon to the city of Athens in Greece. He made the **epic** 26-mile (42 km) run to announce that the Greeks had **defeated** the **Persian** army. Soon after delivering the news, Pheidippides died of exhaustion. Not only had he run the marathon distance, but he had also covered a staggering 150 miles (241 km) running from Athens to Sparta to seek help for the battle. In honor of the **legendary** run that Pheidippides made, in 1896, the organizers of the first modern Olympic Games named the long-distance run "the marathon."

Some endurance runs cross deserts or mountains.

7

MIND AND BODY

Ultramarathons are so tough on the body that people can have **hallucinations** while running. As well as mental difficulties, ultrarunners often experience all kinds of physical problems, from torn muscles to complete exhaustion and collapse.

LOVE TO WIN, LOVE TO RUN

With such a high price to pay, why do runners take on these ultra challenges? Many do it to feel the satisfaction of pushing their bodies to the limit and a sense of huge achievement from accomplishing something that is incredibly difficult to do. Others do it because they simply love running—a lot!

EXTREME STAR

LONG-DISTANCE WARRIOR

One ultrarunner who truly loves running is Courtney Dauwalter. The US athlete is one of the greatest ultrarunners in the world, battling the longest runs, breaking records, and setting new ones that challenge the toughest competitors in the field.

SCHOOL SPORTS STAR

Courtney was born in 1985 in Hopkins, Minnesota. As a child, it seemed she would head into cross-country skiing as her main sport, and she loved to compete in **Nordic** and cross-country ski events. But Courtney also excelled in another sport—running. She ran for her school cross-country team and did so for her university, too.

The Ultra-Trail du Mont-Blanc includes 32,808 feet (10,000 m) of **positive elevation gain**.

COURTNEY SAYS THAT SHE IS **INSTINCTIVE** WHEN IT COMES TO RUNNING AND TRAINING—SHE LISTENS TO HER BODY AND GOES WHERE HER FEET TAKE HER.

COURTNEY TURNS PRO

Courtney studied to become a teacher but all the while, she carried on with her passion—long-distance running. Courtney ran her first ultramarathon in 2011 and won her first medal in 2014. Then, in 2017, she gave up teaching to become a **professional** runner, and she has never looked back.

LAST WOMAN STANDING

Perhaps Courtney's biggest achievement is that she holds the record for the longest distance ever run by a woman in the Big Dog's Backyard Ultra, which is one of the toughest runs in the world. It is a last-man-or-woman standing race in which runners have to complete a distance of just over 4.16 miles (6.7 km) in less than an hour—as many times as they can! Every time a runner completes a lap within an hour, they rest until the next hour's run begins. They run, rest, and repeat over and over, until they literally drop! In 2020, Courtney ran 68 laps—that is 283.3 miles (455.9 km)—with a total lap time of 56 hours, 52 minutes, and 29 seconds!

For ultrarunners like Courtney, training the mind to not give in, even when exhaustion hits, helps get them through their runs.

RUNNING FREE

Have you ever seen a runner run along the sidewalk, leap up onto the side of a building, then run along a wall before somersaulting off it onto the ground? If you have, you've seen a free runner in action!

PARKOUR PLAYGROUND

Free running developed from another style of extreme running —parkour. This hardcore form of running mixes athletic moves, such as jumps, flips, hurdles, and rolls, with running. Runners often use **urban** areas as their training zone but natural landscapes are also a pull. In these places, trees, boulders, and other obstacles make up the free runner's playground.

EXTREME HISTORY

Parkour first started in France, Europe, shortly before World War I (1914–1918), when a man named Georges Hébert came up with a military training method that involved running, jumping, climbing, balancing, swimming, and defending oneself. The training took place on obstacle courses and was designed to make French soldiers prepared for battle.

In the 1950s, a Frenchman named Raymond Belle learned the method during his military training and developed it when he became an elite firefighter. He then passed on his training to his son David Belle. David came up with his own moves, along with a group of friends, in the 1990s. They named themselves the Yamakasi, and wowed crowds with their show-stopping skills.

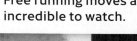
Free running moves are incredible to watch.

Most free runners say they practice the sport so often that they know their limitations and avoid moves that are too dangerous.

"RUNNING —IT SETS MY MIND FREE."

THE SAME BUT DIFFERENT

In parkour, runners aim to get from one place to another as quickly and **efficiently** as possible. They run, climb, swing, **vault**, jump, and roll across anything in their way. Free running is a little different. In this extreme sport, runners aim to impress with their moves, as well as use them to get over obstacles. The climbs, swings, vaults, and rolls they perform are not just about getting over things—but doing it in the most amazing and artistic way possible.

RISKY RUNNING

Like all extreme sports, free running and parkour have their dangers. Falling off objects, especially from high up, can result in bruises and breaks to bones. Runners train to learn how to fall and land as safely as possible to reduce the risk of injury while performing.

THE WORLD'S TOUGHEST RUNS

For elite long-distance runners, Earth's toughest landscapes are a runner's dream. Here are some of the top ultraruns on their bucket list.

Comrades Marathon

Where: Between Durban and Pietermaritzburg, South Africa

The draw: more than 100 years old, this race changes direction every year

Marathon des Sables

Where: The Sahara, Morocco

The draw: a 156-mile (251 km) run across the grueling Sahara. Runners claim it is the world's toughest race

Spartathlon

Where: Greece

The draw: this 153-mile (246 km) race takes runners on the lengthy run made by Pheidippides, from Athens to the ancient site of Sparta

Lapland Arctic Ultra

Where: Sweden

The draw: the **Northern Lights**, rivers, lakes, and mountains in this 311-mile (500 km) run across one of Europe's last areas of wilderness

Ultra-Trail du Mont-Blanc

Where: France, Italy, and Switzerland

The draw: a beautiful 106-mile (171 km) run through breathtaking **alpine** scenery

Dragon's Back Race

Where: Wales

The draw: to run 236 miles (380 km) from the north to the south of Wales with a total **ascent** that is twice the height of Mount Everest!

Fire and Ice Ultra

Where: Iceland

The draw: another spectacular European run, this time 155 miles (250 km) past **lava fields** and **volcanoes**

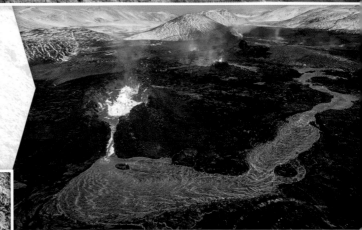

CHAPTER 2

REACHING HIGH

For some extreme land sports lovers, getting up high is the goal. On the world's mountains, some of the most awe-inspiring sports take place. Our planet's peaks draw sportspeople from around the world, who seek out the thrills—and dangers—that mountains hold. From mountaineering and rock climbing to free climbing and abseiling, the planet's rooftop is the only place to be.

TO THE TOP

Mountaineering is the sport of walking or climbing up a mountain in order to reach the summit, or the top. For mountaineers, reaching the summit of a mountain has an irresistible draw. For them, reaching that highest point makes every difficult step and painful breath on the way up worth it.

DANGER ZONE

Mountaineering can be dangerous and scary because it comes with a number of hazards, including the possibility of poor and dangerous weather, falling off the mountainside, and life-threatening **avalanches**.

Reaching the summit of a mountain involves skill, training, and a lot of determination.

"THE TOUGHEST CLIMBS MAKE FOR THE BEST VIEWS IN THE WORLD."

LIGHT AND HEAVY

There are two main types of mountaineering: alpine and expedition. Alpine mountaineering involves climbing medium-sized mountains relatively quickly and with relatively light backpacks. Expedition mountaineering requires carrying a heavier load in the backpack, because trips are longer and mountaineers must therefore take more with them. The mountains climbed in **expeditions** are bigger, often more challenging, and usually more dangerous, too.

DEADLY UP HIGH

Mountaineers face many dangers when climbing. They can fall off the side of a mountain, resulting in injury, and sometimes, death. Crevasses are also a hazard. They are deep cracks in the ice, which are sometimes covered with snow. Falling into a crevasse is a huge problem. Weather on a mountain can quickly change too, bringing storms and lightning. And avalanches are always a danger during climbs in the snow.

Avalanches hold a huge fear for mountain climbers, and for good reason—they can be deadly.

EXTREME HISTORY

People have been climbing mountains for thousands of years. They climbed to travel up and over mountains in order to get from one place to another. Climbing as a sport did not really begin until the eighteenth century, and then boomed during the twentieth century. It was then that famous climbers, such as Sir Edmund Hillary and his guide Tenzing Norgay, made conquering the world's greatest mountains their mission, with Mount Everest being the biggest prize of all. In 1953, Hillary and Norgay made history by reaching the summit of Mount Everest.

MIGHTIEST OF ALL

For many mountaineers, few mountain ranges have as big an appeal as Asia's Himalaya mountain range. This enormous span of mountains contains extreme challenges, and stretches for 1,491 miles (2,400 km) through many countries, including India, Pakistan, China, Bhutan, and Nepal.

KING OF MOUNTAINS

Of all Himalayan mountains, the most famous is Mount Everest. This enormous mountain is the tallest in the world, reaching an incredible 29,029 feet (8,848 m) high. Every year, hundreds of climbers try to reach its summit. The mountain is known to be **treacherous**, and many climbers have died trying to conquer it. Their bodies remain on the mountainside.

Getting to the summit of Mount Everest is a lifelong dream for many climbers.

EXTREME NEED TO KNOW

Climbing Earth's highest mountains takes time. Climbers often complete mountain climbs over a number of weeks, hiking from the bottom, or base, of a mountain to a series of stops, called camps. At each camp, climbers rest and allow their bodies to become used to the increase in altitude, or height. This process is called acclimatization.

MALLORY AND THE MOUNTAIN

George Mallory is one of the most famous mountaineers of all time, and one of the many to find climbing Mount Everest irresistible. Born in England in 1886, Mallory first climbed in the Alps while a student, and soon developed a passion for the sport.

THE CATLIKE CLIMBER

From the outset, it was very clear that Mallory was a natural climber, finding new ways to climb and new routes almost effortlessly. He was described as climbing with the ease of a cat. Mallory joined a number of expeditions to Everest, to try and climb its heights. Each attempt was dangerous and had its own challenges, with some resulting in the death of fellow climbers.

THE BIG PUSH

Despite the difficulties, he was determined not to give up on his Everest dream. In 1924, Mallory set off again for the mountain's peak, this time with a new, young climber named Andrew Irvine. The pair began their push for the summit on June 8. They were said to have last been seen climbing in the early afternoon, after which they were never seen again.

FINDING MALLORY

For years afterward, no one knew what had happened to Mallory and Irvine, or if they had ever made it to Everest's top. Finally, in 1999, a search for the climbers resulted in the discovery of Mallory's body on the mountainside. On examination of the body, it seemed that Mallory had fallen. Many people believe that Mallory and Irvine did make it to the summit of Everest, and were the first to conquer this king of mountains.

George Mallory's body was found just below the ridge to the left of the summit in this picture.

WHEN ASKED WHY HE WANTED TO CLIMB MOUNT EVEREST, MALLORY FAMOUSLY REPLIED "BECAUSE IT'S THERE!"

ROCK CLIMBING

Mountaineering often involves rock climbing, but the activity is also a sport in its own right. Rock climbing involves climbing up steep rocky ground, cliffs, or boulders, but not necessarily to the summit of a mountain. It can even be done indoors on a climbing wall.

MINIMIZE RISKS

When climbing near the ground, when bouldering, for example, climbers do not need to use a safety rope, but may use a mat on the ground so that the risk of injury is reduced. However, when climbing higher, a rope attached to a harness is used. Climbers thread their rope through clips, called carabiners, which then connect to an anchor that the lead climber attaches to the rock. On popular climbs, anchors are sometimes already in place.

EXTREME
NEED TO KNOW

Experienced climbers sometimes climb alone, but most climb with a partner. As one person climbs, their partner remains still and holds the rope securely. By doing so, if the first climber falls, their partner can break the fall by using special equipment that locks the rope. That stops their partner falling too far.

When rock climbing, helmets should always be worn for protection against falling rocks.

"ENJOY THE AIR AND LOOK AT THE VIEW."

Maintaining three points of contact is a golden rule for rock climbers.

BUILT TO CLIMB

Rock climbers have great upper body strength—pulling your own body weight up the side of a mountain builds serious muscle! But just as important as strong muscle is skill. Climbers must **negotiate** difficult **rock formations**, including treacherous **overhangs**, which challenge even the most skilled of climbers.

STRENGTH, SKILL, AND KEEPING STEADY

Along with strength and skill, balance is also a key tool in a climber's kit. Climbers must balance their body weight over their feet as directly as possible to keep steady. An upright position also helps climbers look up a cliff face, seeking out any handholds and footholds on their route upward.

MAKING CONTACT

Keeping three points of contact with the rock is a climbing must, whether that is two hands and a foot, or two feet and one hand. Very rarely will climbers jump from one point to another, but when absolutely necessary, these spectacular moves are needed to travel over especially difficult areas.

TO THE NEXT LEVEL

When mountaineering or rock climbing, many challenges have to be faced such as a crevasse or an overhang. Sometimes, fixed ropes or ladders are already in place to help climbers. However, to climb without any help at all, you must free climb.

FEELING FREE

Free climbers do not use equipment to help them. They climb up the side of a mountain using just their own strength, power, and skill. But they do use gear for protection, such as a rope and carabiners. These important pieces of equipment hold climbers to the mountain face if they lose their grip on it.

"DON'T BE AFRAID TO FAIL. BE AFRAID NOT TO TRY."

Free soloing can be spectacular—and scary—to watch.

The first climber in a group of climbers, or lead climber, will usually free climb.

GOING SOLO

There are some free climbers who really go out on a limb. Free soloing involves climbing with absolutely no gear at all—not even a safety rope. It is by far the most dangerous form of climbing because if the climber makes just a single mistake, it can mean certain death.

EXTREME STARS

KINGS OF CLIMBING

Dean Potter of the United States was one of the most famous free climbers in the world. The gifted athlete was a **BASE jumper** and **highliner**, but was best known for his amazing free climbing skills.

COLLEGE CLIMBER

Always athletic, Dean taught himself to climb while he was in tenth grade, and carried on his climbing passion when he went to university. Climbing held such a draw for Dean that he quit college before graduating to climb full-time.

AN INSPIRATION

Dean inspired other climbers with his incredible skills. He found new routes and carried out amazing solo climbs in Yosemite, California, and Patagonia in South America. He even free-solo climbed part of the super-challenging El Capitan mountain in Yosemite,

creating a new route for climbers, which he then named Easy Rider. Tragically, Dean died in 2015, when the climber attempted a **wingsuit** flight from Taft Point in Yosemite.

ON-FIRE FREE CLIMBING

Another of the world's most amazing free climbers is Alex Honnold. He has made some of the toughest climbs, without any safety equipment, and at incredible and jaw-dropping speed.

TAKING ON THE TRIPLE

Alex set the climbing world on fire when he climbed Half Dome, a famous climb in Yosemite National Park, in 2008. He has since sped up the Yosemite Triple Crown in 18 hours, 50 minutes. That's pretty incredible when you consider that the Triple Crown is made up of three challenging climbing routes: Mount Watkins, The Nose, and the northwest face of Half Dome!

MAKING THE JUMP

Once the summit of a mountain has been reached, there is only one thing left to do—go down! For some extreme sportspeople, that is where the fun really begins. Abseiling is the art of getting quickly down the side of a mountain using a rope, an anchor, and a harness.

ALL CLEAR BELOW

To head downward, an abseiler attaches an anchor to the top of a cliff or another high surface. They always look over the edge that they are going to abseil before beginning a **descent**. This is to check that no one is below them and that the route is clear. They then throw the rope over the edge, and wait for the end to fall to the ground below.

Abseiling is a dangerous sport, in fact, more people die while abseiling than during any other mountaineering activity.

"IT'S THE CLOSEST YOU'LL COME TO FLYING."

FRICTION IS A FRIEND

Next, the abseiler loops the rope through a piece of equipment called a belay device. This device is attached to a harness that the abseiler wears. The belay device is designed to create **friction** between the rope and the belay. This slows down the speed at which the rope moves through the belay, which slows the abseiler's descent.

GOING DOWN

Finally, the abseiler begins to walk off the edge backward. They then move down a cliff or mountain face, bouncing off the side of it with their feet as they descend. All the time, they hold on to the rope, leaning backward and allowing it to move through the belay device as they lower themselves. They keep bouncing and belaying until they reach the ground below.

Abseiling is also called rappelling.

EXTREME NEED TO KNOW

For some extreme sportspeople, abseiling feet-first just isn't edgy enough! They add even more of an **adrenaline** rush to their experience by going headfirst! Some abseilers like to add speed to their drop, descending at an incredible rate. The fastest recorded abseil in the world is 328 feet (100 m) in just 8.99 seconds!

THE WORLD'S MEANEST MOUNTAINS

For elite mountain climbers, Earth has plenty of challenging climbs. But some monster mountains are just meaner than others. These tick all the boxes.

Denali

Where: Alaska, United States

The dangers: remoteness, crevasses and extreme base-to-summit height gain make North America's highest mountain a tough challenge

K2

Where: China and Pakistan

The dangers: the second-tallest mountain in the world, K2 is famous for its deadly seracs—large pillars of ice that can topple and kill climbers

Mount Everest

Where: Nepal and China

The dangers: bad weather, altitude, and avalanches make Everest a dangerous and often-deadly expedition

Cerro Torre

Where: Argentina and Chile

The dangers: dangerous ice and battering winds along with difficult overhangs make this mountain a serious climb

Matterhorn

Where: Switzerland and Italy

The dangers: coming down! Even the easiest route takes longer to descend than ascend and fatigue can be fatal

Annapurna

Where: Nepal

The dangers: this mountain is particularly difficult and dangerous to climb—almost 20 percent of climbers who attempt it die doing so

Baintha Brakk

Where: Pakistan

The dangers: huge and very difficult to climb, only a handful of climbers have ever reached the summit of the mountain known as "the ogre"

CHAPTER 3

BOARD IT, SKATE IT

When it comes to moving across Earth's surface with speed, there are plenty of extreme sport options. From skateboarding and mountain biking through sandboarding and aggressive in-line skating—wheels and extreme sports were made for each other.

THE ULTIMATE URBAN SPORT

Skateboarding is a useful way to get around, and people skate to get from A to B. But extreme skateboarders do more than that—they turn skating into an art. These skateboarders spin and jump on their boards, flip them, ride them on rails, and jump them over obstacles in incredible displays of skill.

RIDING THE RAMP

Skateboarding falls into two main camps—vertical and street. Vertical boarding takes place on a ramp called a halfpipe, so-named because it is shaped like a U. Riders sail from one side of the U to the other on their boards, moving faster and faster until they fly up into the air. Mid-air tricks are incredible to watch.

TAKING IT TO THE STREET

Street skateboarding is just as it sounds—performed on the street, where skateboarders show off their tricks on stairs, rails, and just about any other urban obstacle.

 Skateboarding is one of the most popular urban sports—go to any town or city, and you'll find skaters, skateboarders, and skateparks.

EXTREME HISTORY

Skateboarding has a much longer history than you might think—it first began way back in the 1900s! At that time, budding extreme sports lovers started to put wheels on boards, and ride them—and the skateboard was born. Things slowly moved along until in the 1960s, when **entrepreneurs** saw there was money to be made from making skateboards, and the industry boomed. Soon, skateboarding became a hugely popular sport, and skateboarders started to take stunts and epic moves to the extreme.

Riding a halfpipe takes practice, patience, and padding! Falls happen, and when they do, protective gear makes them a lot less painful.

"SKATEBOARDING IS LIKE LIFE—IF YOU FALL, YOU JUST PICK YOURSELF UP AND TRY AGAIN."

EXTREME WINS

Today, skateboarding is so big that skateboarders prove their worth in competitions. The best known are the X Games and World Skateboarding Championships, and boarders from all over the world take part in these major events.

Competitive skateboarding is big business, with events taking place across the globe.

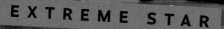
EXTREME STAR

SKATE CHAMPION

Nyjah Huston has won the X Games 13 times, the World Skateboarding Championships 6 times, and has countless other titles to his name.

BABY SKATEBOARDER

The skateboarding star didn't rise to fame and fortune without hard work. He put in the time and put in the practice—starting when he was just four years old. Nyjah had a solid skateboarding start because his parents ran a skatepark in California. His dad was a talented skateboarder and taught his son all that he knew.

PRACTICE PAYS

As a youngster, Nyjah spent some serious time on his sport—up to five hours a day. He soon became an amazing skateboarder, practicing phenomenal tricks time after time.

Nyjah's hard work has paid off because he is considered one of the best in the world—and the most highly paid!

GOING LONG

In all extreme sports, people like to push to the limits, both as sportspeople and as equipment designers. And skateboarding is no exception. Skateboard designers took their boards to an extreme and developed a longboard, to make for an easier ride.

CRUISING SPEED

Longboards are usually around 36 inches (91 cm) long, but can be up to 60 inches (152 cm) in length.

They are also often wider than standard skateboards, which makes them easier to ride. They are ideal for covering long distances, with riders simply cruising along.

DOWNHILL RUN

As in standard skateboarding, longboard riders perform tricks on the board. They also slalom ride on the boards, weaving between obstacles on a course. Downhill riding is the most dramatic way to ride a longboard—riders can reach incredible speeds.

NYJAH SAYS THAT THE CHALLENGES OF SKATEBOARDING MAKE THE SPORT FUN—THERE IS ALWAYS SOMETHING NEW TO TRY.

Longboard skaters can travel up to 80 miles per hour (129 kph)!

THE WORLD'S BEST PARKS

Skateparks are a skateboarder's playground, full of ramps, rails, steps, and just about anything a skater needs to push their sport to the extreme. Here are the top picks.

Skatepark de Los Reyes

Where: Santiago, Chile

The draw: a huge snake run and street skateboarding section with banks, rails, ramps, and stairs

Venice Beach Skatepark

Where: Los Angeles, California

The draw: full of ramps, steps, and platforms, this is considered the home of modern skateboarding

Marseille Skatepark

Where: Marseille, France

The draw: a stunning skatepark often used in movies and the favorite of skateboarding greats

Stoke Plaza

Where: Stoke-on-Trent, England

The draw: a street skater's dream, filled with rails, stairs, ledges, banks, and three bowls that join in the middle

Black Pearl Skate

Where: Cayman Islands

The draw: has 62,000 square feet (5,760 sq m) of pipes, rails, stairs, and bowls

Kona Skatepark

Where: Jacksonville, Florida

The draw: the world's oldest skatepark still in use, it has hills, ramps, and an amazing snake run

Guangzhou Skatepark

Where: Guangzhou, China

The draw: this superskatepark is the biggest in the world and offers vertical skating, pool skating, bowl skating, street skating, and course skating

MOUNTAIN MEETS BOARD

Mountainboarders speed across Earth's surface on a board with wheels, just like skateboarders, but they head for the hills—for some serious downhill action.

JUST ABOUT ANYWHERE

Mountainboards are **versatile**—they can cross all types of terrain, including rocky ground, dirt tracks, concrete surfaces, and grass. That makes them perfect for off-road boarding. Tracks with obstacles are great for weaving, dodging, and jumping!

BUILT TO BE TOUGH

A mountainboard is a little like a cross between a skateboard and a snowboard, with bindings that hold the boarder's feet to the board. The board curves upward at either end. The wheels are designed for tough terrain. They are big and very sturdy—they need to be able to deal with the bumpy, rocky, and ultra-rough surfaces they head down. Two steering devices called trucks are built into the board to help the rider steer left or right as they travel.

Extreme mountainboarders seek out challenging routes, including steep downhill tracks.

EXTREME HISTORY

Mountainboarding was born in the late 1980s and 1990s by snowboarders who wanted to board down mountains even when there was no snow. To fix the problem, they took their snowboards and added wheels—and the mountainboard was born.

BORN TO BOARD

A mountainboarding **legend**, England's Tom Kirkman grew up with outdoor sports, but his love affair with boarding really began when he was a teenager. At just 13 years old, Tom started a small skateboarding store with his father. Skateboarding was Tom's passion until after a year of running the store, he began to sell mountainboards, too. Then, mountainboarding quickly became Tom's go-to sport, and he has never looked back.

FASTER AND HIGHER

Tom learned his mountainboarding craft by boarding in the woods and on the hills near his home. Despite being younger than most other boarders around him, Tom was soon going faster and jumping higher than anyone else!

ONE OF BOARDING'S BEST

It was clear that Tom was set for boarding superstardom, and by the time he was just 19 years old, Tom had been crowned three times World Champion. Today, he is still considered one of the best in the world.

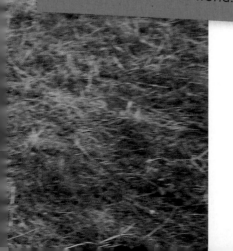

Tom is famous for his spectacular jumps!

TOM SAYS HE TRAINS SIMPLY BY HAVING FUN AND DOING WHAT HE LOVES BEST—MOUNTAINBOARDING!

SURFER'S PARADISE

For some boarders, mountains are great, but sand dunes are even better! They "surf" over the sand on boards. How? By adding a kite! Sand kiters take their sport to the beach, sand dunes, and even the desert. On a super windy day, with wind speeds of 40 miles per hour (64 kph) or more, kiters capture the power of the wind to move them across the sand at incredible speeds. And on the way, they make amazing jumps into the air.

YOUNG AND FRESH

Sand kiting is a young board sport, and boarders are finding new ways all the time to change it up. They add new tricks and moves, and some even surf without a kite. They just head downhill on the sand and let the power of **gravity** do its thing.

Sand kiters can ride over the dunes, but why ride when you can fly?

Sand surfing without a kite is called sandboarding.

SKATING ON THE EDGE

Rollerblading is a fun sport. But for some skaters, the need to go fast adds another, more extreme, edge to the sport. They are called aggressive in-line skaters, and when they put on a pair of blades, they are looking for more than a gentle roll through a park.

Aggressive in-line skaters push the boundaries of their sport to hit faster speeds and make bigger and better jumps.

SOUNDS AGGRESSIVE?

Aggressive in-line skating sounds, well, aggressive! But, it isn't—it simply means a type of skating that is very fast and challenging. Skaters show off amazing tricks on their wheels, from grinds, spins, and jumps to flips and slides. The aim is to impress, and push the sport to its limits.

SKATEPARK SKATERS

Like skateboarders, in-line skaters use skateparks to have fun with their sport. Halfpipes in the parks are great for building up speed on a pair of blades, and a skatepark is the perfect place to try new stunts.

EXTREME NEED TO KNOW

Aggressive in-line skating is a tough sport, so it needs tough equipment. Skates have wheels that are built to handle hard hits when they meet the ground after a jump or race across it at speed. The boots attached to the wheels are tough, too. They have extra, inbuilt support to protect the skater's ankles as they take on stunts.

THE WORLD'S TOP SAND SURFS

Sandboarding is becoming more and more popular as extreme sports lovers discover that surfing on land can be as fun as surfing on water. Here are a sandboarder's top picks.

Monte Kaolino

Where: Germany

The rush: Monte Kaolino is one of the largest sand hills in Europe. It has dunes up to 492 feet (150 m) tall. A lift takes boarders to the top

Sand Master Park

Where: Oregon, United States

The rush: great for beginners—once skills are mastered, the Oregon coast has the best dunes in the country

Little Sahara

Where: Kangaroo Island, Australia

The rush: another great place for **newbies**, the dunes cover 1.2 square miles (3.1 sq km)

Swakopmund and Walvis Bay

Where: Namibia

The rush: rich, golden sand that is perfect for surfing, on the edge of the Namib Desert

Huacachina Oasis

Where: Peru

The rush: very tall sand dunes—some of the tallest in the world—with fine, golden sand and beautiful views

Badain Jaran Desert

Where: China

The rush: some of the tallest dunes in the world—and they also sing! When the wind blows away the top layer of sand, it creates an **electrostatic charge** in the lower layers, making a low-frequency noise

Taboga Beach

Where: Morocco

The rush: a stunning set of golden sand dunes, situated right next to the sea

CHAPTER 4

LIFE MEANS BIKE!

Cycling is one of the most popular sports in the world, with many people riding a bike for fitness, fun, or simply to get from A to B. For elite cyclists, cycling is their world, and they live to bike.

HITTING THE ROAD HARD

Like long-distance running, long-distance road cycling is an endurance sport that requires extreme training, extreme fitness, and extreme commitment. Elite long-distance cyclists get on their bikes day after day, covering many miles on the road every time.

THE ORIGINAL EXTREME SPORT

Of all long-distance cycling events, one is considered the toughest of all—the Tour de France. This world-famous race is even believed to be the most difficult sporting event in the world, with riders racing for a staggering three weeks. For many, the Tour de France is the original extreme sport.

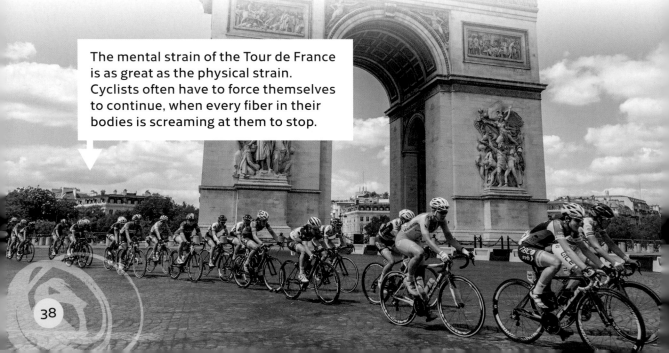

The mental strain of the Tour de France is as great as the physical strain. Cyclists often have to force themselves to continue, when every fiber in their bodies is screaming at them to stop.

The Tour de France is known to be dangerous, too, with injuries often occurring if cyclists crash into each other accidentally or lose their grip on the road.

DAY AFTER DAY

During the Tour, cyclists must complete 21 grueling stages, one each day with one or two rest days. By the end of the Tour, riders have covered a staggering 2,277 miles (3,664 km). And like the race's name suggests, much of it is through some of France's hilliest terrain. The toughest stage is called the Queen stage and passes through the French Alps, with supersteep climbs that push cyclists to the limits of their endurance.

BRUTAL TO BODIES

Every day, cyclists on the Tour burn around 5,000 calories, which is almost twice as much as a marathon runner might burn during a race. All the time too, cyclists must keep their minds alert, watching out for other cyclists, difficult bends in the road, changes in terrain, and **spectators**, who can sometimes cause accidents.

HEADING OFF ROAD

Along with road cycling, bicycle motocross (BMX) is also a favorite with many extreme sportspeople. BMX bikes are smaller and tougher than road bikes, and are designed to pull amazing stunts and tricks. Bikers often **customize** their bikes, taking away and adding parts to suit their style of riding.

EXTREME EXPLORERS

For some cyclists, heading out on their bikes into the world's wildest places is the biggest draw of all. Mountain biking, known as MTB, involves off-road riding through often-treacherous terrain, such as rocky landscapes and mountainous areas. Riders use bikes that are specially designed for the ultra-challenging places they ride in.

TYPES OF BIKING

There are different types of MTB, including trail, cross-country (XC), downhill (DH), and Enduro. Trail riding is fairly gentle and takes place on marked trails. XC involves completing a course, sometimes on trails and sometimes on roads, often with obstacles. DH is all about going downhill—fast!

Races, stunts, big air, and crowds—it's all BMX!

Mountain bikes have big, wide, and tough wheels that can take traveling over rocky terrain.

40

MIXING IT UP

Enduro is a mix of XC and DH. It takes place on off-road terrain with obstacles, up or down a mountain. The races consist of several timed stages, mostly the downhills are timed, with sections known as liaisons in-between. These liaison sections join the end of one stage to the start of another.

EXTREME STAR

THE CROSS-COUNTRY CANADIAN

Emily Batty is a Canadian XC star! Emily grew up surrounded by bikes and riders in a diehard XC racing family. Her two elder brothers both race, so too does her younger sister.

FROM FARM TO FAMOUS

Emily and her siblings spent their days mountain biking across their farm in Ontario, where they honed their skills. As she grew older, Emily's talent was clear for all to see, and it soon turned into an incredible career.

CHALLENGES AND CHAMPIONSHIPS

Emily began racing seriously in 1999, and went on to compete in a series of challenges, smashing it every time. Emily has never let injury hold her back and she even competed at the 2012 Summer Olympics with a broken collarbone! She went on to win many titles, including bronze at the 2016 and 2018 World Championships.

Before her retirement in 2023, Emily was the Pan American Games champion.

THE WORLD'S ULTIMATE MTB TRAILS

There are some incredible MTB trails around the world, where the views and the jumps combine for the ultimate rides. For elite riders, these are the world's best.

Yungas Road

Where: Bolivia

The draw: also known as the "death road," the route has a massive 40-mile (64 km) downhill dirt track, with sheer drops

The Cliffs of Moher

Where: Ireland

The draw: the ride is a ledge on a sheer cliff face above the Atlantic Ocean, and is just a few feet wide —probably for that reason, it is now illegal to ride there

Radwanderung Trail

Where: Austria

The draw: a steep and narrow track through a **gorge**—riders need skills and concentration

The Ridge

Where: Isle of Skye, Scotland

The draw: a seemingly impossible ride on the wild Cuillin Ridge, with jagged trails, often-stormy weather, and incredibly challenging terrain

The White Line

Where: Arizona, United States

The draw: considered one of the world's scariest rides, this **sandstone** track is on an incredibly steep cliff with an enormous drop below

Porcupine Rim

Where: Utah, United States

The draw: this ride has 3 miles (4.8 km) of treacherous riding with sheer cliffs that drop to the Colorado River below

Higher Maritime Alps

Where: France

The draw: supersteep climbs, demanding riding, and amazing views

EXTREME GLOSSARY

abseil to travel down a vertical or near-vertical surface using a rope

adrenaline a hormone, or chemical messenger in the body, that creates a sense of excitement and a surge of energy

alpine describes high mountainous regions, particularly the Alps in Europe

ascent an upward journey, usually on a mountain

athletes people who take part in sports, often competing at a high level

avalanches often violent movements of snow, ice, and rock down a slope

BASE jumper a person who takes part in the extreme sport of BASE jumping. BASE jumping, which involves parachuting or wingsuit flying from fixed objects, such as buildings, antennas, bridges, or cliffs

customize modify or change to suit a particular individual or task

defeated beaten

descent a downward journey, usually on a mountain

deserts very dry places with little or no rainfall

efficiently carrying out a task or achieving a goal with minimal waste or effort

electrostatic charge electric energy that builds up on an object

elite the best at something

endurance able to do something, such as a physical activity, for a long time

entrepreneur a person who sets up a business taking on financial risks in the hope of making a profit

epic describes something that is very impressive and extraordinary

expedition an organized journey for a particular purpose

extreme sports high-risk sports that push sportspeople to their limits

friction resistance created when two objects come into contact and move against each other. Friction generates heat and can cause objects to slow down or stop

frontier a boundary or border that marks the outer limits of settled or known areas

gorge a narrow valley between hills or mountains, usually with steep rocky walls and a stream running through it

gravity the force that pulls objects toward other large objects

grueling extremely demanding and exhausting

hallucinations things that appear real but are not

highliner a person who takes part in the extreme sport of highlining, which involves walking or balancing on a narrow, suspended line stretched between two anchor points at a considerable height

instinctive describes behaving or responding in a way that is based on how a person feels

lava fields areas covered by hardened lava resulting from volcanic eruptions. Lava fields usually have rugged and rocky ground

legend a term often used to describe a person whose achievements are extremely great

legendary describes something that is part of an extraordinary story, and is often associated with a remarkable accomplishment

negotiate to successfully find a way around an obstacle or through a difficult route

newbies people who are beginners or new to something

Nordic describes the people, cultures, or languages of Northern European countries, particularly those of Scandinavia, which includes Sweden, Norway, Finland, and Denmark

Northern Lights also known as the Aurora Borealis, these natural light displays occur in Earth's polar regions. They are caused by the interaction between solar particles and Earth's magnetic field, resulting in colorful and shimmering lights in the sky

overhangs sections of rock or terrain that extend horizontally or diagonally beyond a vertical or near-vertical surface. Overhangs are very challenging for climbers and require specialized techniques to overcome

Persian refers to the country of Persia, which is modern-day Iran

positive elevation gain the distance above the height from where you started. Negative elevation is the distance below where you started

professional describes a person who does a sport or another activity as a way of earning money

remoteness being far away from other things or people

rock formations natural structures or arrangements of rocks, often shaped over long periods of time

sandstone a rock made up of sand-sized grains of mineral, rock, or other material. Sandstone often has many little holes and different colors

scale the act of climbing a vertical or steep surface

spectators people who watch an event or performance

terrain the physical characteristics of a particular area of land. Terrain can range from flat and open to rugged and mountainous

trails marked paths or routes often used for hiking, biking, or other outdoor activities

treacherous describes something that is full of danger

urban describes cities, towns, or other areas with many buildings and people

vault to leap or jump over an obstacle

venture to explore or take on a daring exploration

versatile describes something that can be used in various ways or for different purposes

volcanoes openings in the Earth's crust through which melted rock, gases, and ash are thrown out during volcanic eruptions. Volcanoes are usually cone-shaped mountains or hills

wingsuit a specialized jumpsuit with fabric wings that allow a person to glide through the air after jumping from a high point, such as a mountain or aircraft

FIND OUT MORE

BOOKS

DISCOVER MORE ABOUT EXTREME SPORTS WITH THESE GREAT READS.

Bramucci, Steve. *Rock Stars!: True Stories of Extreme Climbing Adventures!* (Chapters). National Geographic Kids, 2018.

Drake, Raelyn. *Off Road* (To the Limit). Derby Creek, 2019.

Payment, Simone. *Extreme Rock Climbing* (Extreme Sports and Stunts). Rosen Publishing, 2020.

Stevenson, Paul. *Parkour* (Buzz Books). Hungry Tomato, 2023.

Vescia, Monique. *Extreme Parkour* (Extreme Sports and Stunts). Rosen Publishing, 2020.

Wolny, Philip. *Extreme Skateboarding* (Extreme Sports and Stunts). Rosen Publishing, 2020.

WEBSITES AND ORGANIZATIONS

THESE WEBSITES ARE GREAT FOR LEARNING MORE ABOUT THE WORLD OF LAND SPORTS, AND IF YOU WANT TO TRY YOUR HAND AT SOME OF THEM, YOU CAN START YOUR JOURNEY HERE.

Find out more about climbing courses and programs for climbers of all levels at the American Alpine Institute (AAI):
www.alpineinstitute.com

Learn more about parkour at:
www.americanparkour.com

Learn more about great mountain bikers and the history of mountain biking at the Mountain Bike Hall of Fame:
www.mmbhof.org/mtn-bike-hall-of-fame

Learn more about skateboarding at The Skatepark Project, founded by the legendary skateboarder Tony Hawk, and discover the mission to build skateparks for young people:
www.skatepark.org

The American Trail Running Association (ATRA) has a lot of information about trail running:
www.trailrunner.com

USA Track & Field (USATF) has a lot of detail about long-distance running events and athletes in the United States:
www.usatf.org

Publisher's note to educators and parents:
All the websites featured above have been carefully reviewed to ensure that they are suitable for students. However, many websites change often, and we cannot guarantee that a site's future contents will continue to meet our high standards of educational value. Please be advised that students should be closely monitored whenever they access the Internet.

INDEX

ABOUT THE AUTHOR

Sarah Eason is an experienced children's book author who has written many books about sport and sport science. She would love to visit some of the amazing places researched while writing this book, and (maybe!) try out some extreme sports there.